ENGLISH
HERALDIC MANUSCRIPTS
IN THE
BRITISH MUSEUM

C. E. WRIGHT
F.S.A.

PUBLISHED FOR THE BRITISH LIBRARY BOARD
BY BRITISH MUSEUM PUBLICATIONS LTD
LONDON
1973

SBN 7141 0484 1

*Printed in Great Britain
at the University Press, Oxford
by Vivian Ridler
Printer to the University*

Preface

★ The purpose of this small book is to offer to those interested in heraldry a brief survey of the English heraldic material in the British Museum's manuscript collections. After an introductory section describing the various kinds of heraldic manuscripts with an account of representative manuscript examples of each, the Department's four nucleus collections, Harley, Cotton, Sloane, and Royal, are examined in that order and then the Lansdowne, Stowe, and Arundel; the survey concludes with an account of the individual items or collections to be found in the Additional and Egerton series.

In the List of Illustrations very full descriptive notes have been supplied for each of the subjects selected for reproduction both in colour and in black and white, and references to these will be found at the appropriate places in the text; in the text itself also cross-references have been inserted wherever the individual items are described or referred to in several places.

The bibliography is a very selective one being intended only to guide the reader to the more important books necessary to supply background to this survey of the Museum's English heraldic manuscripts. The glossary is confined to such terms as appear in the text.

On 1 July 1973 the Department of Manuscripts of the British Museum became part of the British Library but the collections of the Department are still housed in the British Museum.

C. E. WRIGHT

List of Illustrations

4

1. CAERLAVEROCK POEM (OR ROLL) (see p. 8). Contemporary verse account in French of the lords and knights present at Edward I's siege of the castle of Caerlaverock in Dumfriesshire, in July 1300, with blazon of arms. Cotton Caligula A. xviii, f. 26b.

2. PETERBOROUGH ROLL (see p. 8). Shields of arms of the Abbey and three of its tenants (Galfridus de Sancto Medardo, Rogerus de Torpel, Thomas filius Roberti de Gunthorp) painted in the margins of a chronicle and cartulary of Peterborough Abbey by Walter of Whittlesey, *circa* 1321-9. Additional 39758, f. 50.

3. HARLEIAN ROLL (see p. 8). Four from a series of shields of arms painted in the upper margins of a manuscript of a French poem by Guillaume de Waddington entitled 'Manuel des Pechez', temp. Edward II. The shields on the page reproduced are those of La Zouche, Stafford, Crevequer, and Mohun. Harley 337, f. 25b.

4. DERING (A) ROLL (see p. 9). Seven rows of the painted shields of arms from a vellum roll of arms copied in the fifteenth century from the original roll of *circa* 1275. Owned *circa* 1640 by Sir Edward Dering, 1st Bart., who has inserted at the beginning of the third row the fictitious coat of 'Ric. fiz Dering'. Additional 38537.

5. THOMAS JENYNS' BOOK (see p. 9). Queen Margaret's Version. Painted coats of arms arranged for the most part as an Ordinary, executed possibly in the 1440s. Additional 40851, f. 7.

6. PORTCULLIS' BOOK (see p. 11). Miscellaneous collection of painted shields of arms, executed *circa* 1440; so called because at the top of f. 56 is written in a later hand 'Portcullis'. Harley 521, f. 20.

7. STRANGWAYS' BOOK (see pp. 11-12). Treatise on heraldry written by Richard Strangways (d. 1488), of the Inner Temple. The page reproduced shows, boldly drawn and painted, the shield of arms of Sir William Pecche (*az*, a lion rampant double-queued *ermine* crowned *or*) (cf. the Sir William Pecche brass of 1487 and the Sir John Pecche monumental effigy of 1522 in Lullingstone church, Kent). Harley 2259, f. 115b.

8. 'DE OFFICIO MILITARI'. A treatise on rules of war, duties of heralds, etc., composed by Nicholas Upton (d. 1457), Fellow of New College, Oxford, dedicated by him to Humphrey, Duke of Gloucester (see p. 14). The present manuscript was used by Sir Edward Bysshe for his edition published in 1654. Cotton Nero C. iii, f. 65b.

9. BOOK OF HOURS, executed for Sir William Oldhall (d.? 1466), of Narford in Norfolk, and his wife, Margaret, daughter of William, 5th Baron Willoughby de Eresby (see p. 20). In the miniature reproduced, Oldhall is shown kneeling before St. George, his arms being painted on his tabard and on the shield inserted in the capital initial G. Harley 2900, f. 55.

10. BRUGES' GARTER BOOK (see pp. 16-17). A volume containing twenty-six full-page coloured drawings of the Founder Knights of the Garter, of King Edward III, and of Garter King of Arms, executed for William Bruges (d. 1450), first Garter King of Arms, probably *circa* 1430. The figure on the page

illustrated is that of the Duke of Lancaster and the shields in the frame are those of the successors in his stall in St. George's Chapel at Windsor. Stowe 594, f. 8.

11. WRITHE'S GARTER BOOK (see p. 25). A *facsimile copy* made *circa* 1640 for Sir Christopher Hatton of the Garter Armorial compiled by John Writhe (d. 1504), Garter King of Arms, containing paintings of the shields, crests, and badges (some displayed on banners) of Knights of the Garter. The three sovereigns whose badges appear on the page illustrated are Edward III (the sun's rays issuing from a cloud and an ostrich feather, here surmounted by a crown), Richard II (a white hart, gorged with a crown and chained [of which the most beautiful representation is that on the Wilton Diptych], accompanied by the sun in splendour), and Henry IV (a red rose and a fox's tail dependent). Additional 37340, f. 1.

12. FUNERAL COLLECTIONS OF SIR THOMAS WRIOTHESLEY, Garter King of Arms 1505–34 (see p. 25). Description of the funeral ceremony of William Courtenay, 9th Earl of Devon, 1511, with painted drawings of his armorial insignia (shield of arms with mantling, helm, and crest, his banner, and pennon). Additional 45131, f. 67b.

13. SALISBURY ROLL. Leaf from a *copy*, 1483–5, of the Salisbury Roll of Arms (*circa* 1460) showing painted full-length figures of members of the families of the Earls of Salisbury and their wives (see p. 25). The figures are arranged in pairs of a husband and wife linked by a cord or chain, most of the men in armour with a tabard of arms together with shield of arms, helm, and crest beside the figure, and the women wearing a mantle either of their husband's arms or their husband's coat impaling their father's. Above are contemporary inscriptions. The present manuscript is also part of Sir Thomas Wriothesley's heraldic collections. Additional 45133, f. 55.

14. GRANT OF ARMS TO SIR NICHOLAS BACON, Lord Keeper (see p. 27); the arms are painted in the left-hand margin and are: quarterly, 1st and 4th for Bacon, *gu* on a chief *arg* 2 mullets *sa*, 2nd and 3rd Quaplade, barry of six *or* and *az* over all a bend *gu*; with crest, namely, on a torse *arg* and *gu* a boar passant *ermine*, mantled *az*, doubled *or*, with, below, three alternative crests; in the other margins are coats of arms of the Ufford, Quaplade, Ferneley, and Cooke families. Dated 27 February 1568/9. At foot are the signatures (and seals) of Sir Gilbert Dethick, Garter, Robert Cooke, Clarenceux, and William Flower, Norroy, Kings of Arms. In the illuminated initial is a portrait of (?) Sir Gilbert Dethick in crown and tabard. Additional 39249.

15. ANDREW OF WYNTOUN'S 'THE ORYGYNALE CRONYKYL OF SCOTLAND', in verse, a manuscript written and illuminated towards the end of the fifteenth century; a copy formerly in the possession of Sir William Le Neve while York Herald (1625–33) (Clarenceux King of Arms 1635; d. 1661), who has inserted his signatures and painted coat of arms (*arg*, on a cross *sa* 5 fleurs de lis *arg*) on the first leaf, as reproduced (see p. 21). Royal 17 D. xx, f. 1.

16. NOTES OF ARMS AND MONUMENTS IN KENTISH CHURCHES by John Philipot (d. 1645), Somerset Herald 1624, with many drawings of tombs and shields of arms in trick (see p. 27). The page reproduced shows those taken in St. Nicholas's church at Ash-next-Sandwich, 20 November 1613. The monumental effigies alleged to commemorate Sir [John de] Goshall and [Sir John] Leverick are still preserved in the church. Egerton 3310 A, f. 3.

English Heraldic Manuscripts in the British Museum

1

The great accumulation of heraldic manuscripts now preserved in the British Museum is surpassed in size and variety of content only by that in the College of Arms. However, before describing in detail the several individual collections of the Department of Manuscripts in which the heraldic manuscripts are to be found it is essential by way of introduction to define briefly the chief categories of the material that came into being as a result of the heralds' activities and to illustrate each by one or two examples selected from the Museum's holdings.

The heralds' concern with coats of arms arose in the first place quite naturally out of their duties at tournaments and can be traced back to the late twelfth century. The evidence from the oldest rolls of arms, the work of unknown hands, shows that by 1250 at any rate the language of blazon (that is, the terms used to describe the colours of the field and then of the main and subsidiary charges on the shields) had been reduced to a system; at first the language was French and remained so until about 1440 when English begins to appear. By 1350 such rolls of arms were certainly being compiled by heralds; Sir Anthony Wagner, the present Garter King of Arms, has drawn attention to an interesting passage in 'Pierce the Ploughman's Crede', written about 1394, in which the author, after referring to the shields of arms in the windows of a house of Dominicans, adds: 'Ther is non heraud that hath half swich a rolle'—thereby indicating an already accepted connection between the heralds and rolls of arms. These rolls, which may be literally rolls or in book form, fall into several well-defined kinds. Of these, that of the 'Illustrative Rolls' stands perhaps rather apart, as being non-heraldic, being in fact collections of arms painted in chronicles or cartularies primarily by way of illustration. Of this group the earliest known English example is furnished by the shields painted in the margins of manuscripts of his chronicles by Matthew Paris, who died in 1259. In Royal 14 C. vii the Museum possesses what is almost certainly the author's autograph manuscript of his Historia Anglorum with the addition of the Chronica Majora, compiled between 1250 and 1259 and containing in the margins (see also p. 15 below) no less than ninety-five painted shields of persons mentioned in his text, while in another Matthew Paris manuscript in the Museum, the author's original copy of his Abbreviatio Chronicarum, Cotton Claudius D. vi, some folios are similarly adorned with shields (eleven in all); perhaps earlier than either of these manuscripts, however, is a third Matthew Paris item in the Museum, the sheet of arms inserted in the Liber Additamen-torum, Cotton Nero D. i (f. 171), which may have been made *circa* 1244, while the rough drawings of shields on ff. 200, 200b in the same manuscript may be even earlier. Similarly in the earlier of two other examples of Illus-trative Rolls in the Department a chronicle has been used as a basis; this is a manuscript (Additional 39758) of a chronicle and cartulary of Peterborough Abbey made by Walter of Whittlesey about 1321 to 1329, in the margins of a number of leaves in which are painted first the arms of the abbey and then those of sixteen of its tenants (Peterborough Roll) (see Pl. 2).[1] In the second example the upper margins of the folios (12–31) of that part of a manuscript containing William of Waddington's 'Manuel des Pechez', have been decorated with the coats of arms of various knights, one of whom (Sir Giles de Argentein) was killed at the Battle of Bannockburn in 1314; to this collection of shields has been given the title 'Harleian Roll', the manuscript being Harley 337 (see p. 11 and Pl. 3).

It is not surprising, in view of the original function of the heralds, that 'Occasional Rolls' should form a considerable and important group; this is the term applied to a roll recording the arms of the lords and knights present on a particular occasion, the oldest known English example being the Falkirk Roll, a collection of the arms of the English bannerets present at the Battle of Falkirk, fought by Edward I against Wallace on 22 July 1298. The original of this is no longer extant but the Department possesses the transcript of the original (then in the College of Arms) made in 1606 by Nicholas Charles, Lancaster Herald (Harley 6589, ff. 9–9b). Of the next oldest specimen of this class, however, the famous Caerlaverock Roll (or Poem), a coeval account in rhymed-couplets of the lords and knights present at Edward I's siege of the castle of Caerlaverock in Dumfriesshire in July 1300, the Museum possesses the earliest text (with the arms in blazon) in a contemporary or near con-temporary copy in a manuscript in the Cotton Collection—Caligula A. xviii (see Pl. 1). It owns also one well-known later example of this kind, the (Third) Calais Roll (Additional 29502), which was executed about 1348 and contains 'the names off the lordes and captens that weyre sleyn and dront on the sey at the sege of Callas [1345–8] with many a man mo off worschipe'; this roll comprises twenty-four painted shields poorly executed, the red appearing as a rusty brown. It is significant of the haste with which the rolls in this class were made that in all, with the exception of the last named, the arms are blazoned and not painted. The largest class of all of course is that of the 'General Rolls', which begin usually with the sovereigns of the world (from Prester John, the King of Jerusalem, and the Emperor downwards) and continue with the English earls, lords, knights, and esquires, arranged usually in no very clearly explicable order. The Museum's earliest specimen of this group is the Camden Roll of *circa* 1280, a roll preserved in the Cotton collection (Cotton Roll XV. 8) and named after its one-time

[1] It has recently been suggested that 'Feudal Roll' would be a better description of this roll in view of its contents. See J. A. Goodall in *The Coat of Arms*, iv, no. 28 (Oct. 1956), pp. 148–9.

owner, William Camden, the famous antiquary and, from 1597 to his death in 1623, Clarenceux King of Arms; the recto or face of the roll is painted with 270 shields beginning with the arms of the King of Jerusalem, and among the English arms are those of Alphonso ('Sire Aunfons') (no. 26), the eldest son of Edward I who died in August 1284. Early in the fourteenth century the blazon of 185 of these arms was added (in French) on the verso of the roll. The two remaining categories are known as 'Local Rolls' and 'Ordinaries'. An excellent representative of the former kind is the Dering Roll, the original of which *circa* 1275 is now in the possession of Sir Anthony Wagner; it is 'local' in the sense that the shields are for the most part those of Kent and Sussex knights and it derives its name from the fact that it was at one time in the possession of Sir Edward Dering, 1st Bart. (d. 1644), of Surrenden Dering in Kent, antiquary and politician, as was the fifteenth-century copy of this roll which the Museum possesses (Additional 38537) (see Pl. 4): this has the additional interest that it bears evidence of Dering's having tampered with it by inserting a coat of arms for 'Ric. fiz Dering', a fictitious ancestor. (Dering also tampered with the monumental brasses in his parish church at Pluckley.)

A roll of 'Ordinaries' is a collection of arms arranged by design or subject-matter, thus all the coats containing (say) eagles are grouped together. One of the finest specimens of this class is that designated 'Thomas Jenyns' Book', from the fact that one version of it belonged to Thomas Jenyns, a gentleman of the household of Henry, Earl of Huntingdon; this book Jenyns gave to Robert Glover, Somerset Herald, who was in possession of it in 1578 in which year he made the Museum copy, now Stowe 696. An earlier version, also in the Department of Manuscripts, Additional 40851 (see Pl. 5), belonged to Margaret of Anjou, consort of Henry VI, 1445–82, a large shield of her arms being painted at the beginning.

It should be observed that the names attached to these rolls have been given to them in post-medieval times and (apart from the Occasional Rolls which naturally take their names from the 'occasions' for which they were compiled) are usually those of former owners, such as the Camden Roll, or, sometimes, of their first editors, for example, Willement's Roll (Egerton 3713). Authorship of individual heralds is known only from the fifteenth century. The earliest example perhaps is that supplied by the volume known as 'Bruges' Garter Book', a manuscript containing twenty-six full-page coloured drawings of the Founder Knights of the Garter, of King Edward III, and of Garter King of Arms kneeling before St. George, compiled *circa* 1430 by William Bruges, first Garter King of Arms, who died in 1450, and preserved, like Glover's copy of Jenyns' Book referred to above, in the Stowe collection in the Department (Stowe 594) (see Pl. 10). Another instance of a manuscript now bearing the name of a former owner and containing fine coloured drawings is the great heraldic compilation entitled from its association with Sir Thomas Holme, Clarenceux King of Arms 1476–94, as 'Sir Thomas Holme's Book'; of the three collections comprised under that heading the manuscripts of two are preserved in the Museum (namely Harley

4205 (see Pl. I) and Additional 45133). And from the late fifteenth and early sixteenth centuries is preserved a great corpus of heraldic material associated with John Writhe, Garter King of Arms 1478–1504, and with his son and successor, Sir Thomas Wriothesley, Garter King of Arms 1505–38, many volumes of which are in the Museum's possession. From the sixteenth century onwards material of all kinds (such as antiquarian notes compiled on their tours, the so-called 'church notes', drawings of seals, pedigrees) brought together by individual heralds right down to the nineteenth century is preserved in the Department and few if any of the more notable heralds are unrepresented. The Department's heraldic manuscripts include also copies (and in a few instances originals, e.g. Harley 1141, 1163, 1165, which bear the signatures of the gentry to their pedigrees, a practice introduced by Clarenceux Cooke in 1570) of the Visitations which were established on a formal basis in 1530, when Henry VIII issued to Thomas Benolt, Clarenceux, Letters Patent regulating visitations by heralds, and continued until the Revolution of 1688; papers relating to the College of Arms itself (including some of those of Sir William Dugdale, Garter 1677–86); and material relating to the Court of Chivalry, the Order of the Garter, and state ceremonial. While quite in a class of its own is the Rous Roll, a chronicle roll of the Earls of Warwick compiled by John Rous, Chantry Priest of Guy's Cliffe, Warwick, who died in 1491 (see pp. 25–26), the English version of which was acquired by the Museum in 1955 (Additional 48976) (see Pl. III).

2

In any account of the Department's individual collections containing heraldic material pride of place must be given to the Harleian Collection because it contains the largest amount of such material. This was the collection of manuscripts formed originally by Robert Harley, 1st Earl of Oxford (d. 1724), and continuously expanded by his son Edward, the 2nd Earl (d. 1741). Robert Harley had a strong interest in such manuscripts, but the collections (apart from individual items) of this kind that he was able to acquire were mostly those of the seventeenth-century arms painters (men such as John Withie [d.? *circa* 1678], John Saunders [d. *circa* 1687], and Richard Mundy [*fl. circa* 1639]), which though of considerable extent include little notable material though original manuscripts of such heralds as, for example, Nicholas Charles (d. 1613), Sampson Lennard (d. 1633), and William Penson (d. 1637), are to be found in them.

Robert Harley's most important acquisition of this kind (secured through the mediation of Francis Gastrell, Bishop of Chester) was the Randle Holme heraldic and genealogical collection; this had been accumulated by four generations of the Randle Holme family, arms painters of Chester, the last—Randle Holme IV—dying in 1707. At least one important early heraldic manuscript had found a place in this collection, the so-called 'Randle Holme's Book' (Harley 2169), a volume containing pen and colour-wash drawings of crowned, armed, and mounted figures with arms on their shields and trappings, of William I, Henry V, and Henry VI, coats of arms of the Nine

Worthies, of foreign sovereigns, English princes, earls, lords, knights, and gentry, and so on; a shield of arms of 'Warrewyke le herawde', in the manuscript, evidently for David Griffith, Warwick Herald *circa* 1469–80, suggests that he may be the author of the compilation. The Harleian Roll of Edward I's reign (Harley 337, ff. 12–31), referred to above (see p. 8), came to Robert Harley in the library of the antiquary and collector, Sir Simonds D'Ewes (d. 1650), which Harley acquired in 1705; one other early heraldic manuscript 'Portcullis' Book', executed *circa* 1440 (Harley 521) (see Pl. 6), *may* also have been among the contents of D'Ewes's library. Robert Harley's son, Edward, the 2nd Earl, who was chiefly responsible for the everyday conduct of the Library affairs from *circa* 1711, inherited also his father's interest in heraldic manuscripts. We find him writing in 1717 to the Harleian librarian, Humfrey Wanley, 'I shall be glad to make the collection of Heraldical MSS. as compleat as possible'. To this end he kept a watchful eye on the appearance of such manuscripts. Consequently we find him acquiring in 1720 from Christopher Bateman, the London bookseller, the Sir Thomas Holme's Book I (Harley 4205) (see pp. 9–10 and Pl. I), and in 1725 from William Welles, 'watchmaker', the executor of an arms painter, King, a group of original grants of arms which comprise grants by William Camden, Thomas Hawley, Sir Thomas Wriothesley, and Sir Richard St. George (all now incorporated in Harley 7025). And this interest continued throughout Edward Harley's life since as late as 1738 and 1739 he was buying items from Osborne's sales of heraldic material accumulated by the St. George family. The source from which he obtained the well-known volume (Harley 4632) entitled from its former owner and collector, Sir Christopher Barker, Garter King of Arms 1536, 'Barker's Grants', is unknown. The same is true, unfortunately, of several manuscripts almost certainly to be identified as products (like part of Sir Thomas Holme's Book) of the studio which Sir Thomas Wriothesley must have established, probably at the great house called Garter House which he built for himself in Red Cross Street, Cripplegate, on becoming Garter in 1505: such as Harley 1499, the copy of Thomas Tonge's 1530 Visitation of the Northern Counties, and Harley 4900, a collection of copies of patents of creation and grants of arms. The latter has a particularly interesting pedigree of ownership, having passed through the hands of no less than three Garters, namely, the two Dethicks, Sir Gilbert (d. 1584) and his son Sir William (d. 1612), the latter of whom received it as a gift from his father in 1564, and Sir John Borough (d. 1643); and lastly Peter Le Neve, Norroy King of Arms, who was also at one time owner of Harley 6163, a general roll of arms compiled *circa* 1480–1500 and now known as 'Peter Le Neve's Book'; it is related to 'Writhe's Book' and has notes in Writhe's hand. It was earlier in the possession of Sir William Segar (d. 1633), Garter. Peter Le Neve was the donor of many manuscripts to the Harleian Library and in addition a number were purchased from him at various dates; we do not know how Harley 6163 passed into the Library—perhaps it was bought by Edward Harley at Le Neve's sales in 1731. Nor do we know where Harley found the collection of heraldic memoranda made in the 1450s by

Richard Strangways (d. 1488) of the Inner Temple and known as 'Strang-ways' Book' (Harley 2259) (see Pl. 7) from its collector of whom it has been said that, 'As a collector of the queer terms and turns of blazon with which the fifteenth-century theorists befuddled armory Strangways has no rival.'[1] The names of few of the more important pre-eighteenth-century heralds would be lacking in any list of one-time owners of Harley manuscripts.

3

Of the sixteenth- and seventeenth-century antiquary-collectors whose manu-script collections are now in the British Museum much the most outstanding figure was Sir Robert Cotton (1571–1631), whose library (with coins and other antiquities) became the property of the nation on the death of his grandson, Sir John Cotton, in 1702, and one of the nucleus collections of the British Museum at its formation in 1753. Cotton was a Huntingdonshire man born at Denton close to the Northamptonshire border, but his country seat was Conington Castle, whose closely adjoining church contains many Cotton monuments including that erected to him on his own death; in view of his antiquarian enthusiasms it is not without interest to observe that his mother was one of the Shirleys of Staunton Harold in Leicestershire, a family notable for its pride of ancestry and the antiquarian researches of several of its members. Cotton's own interests in the manuscript part of his collections were wide ranging in subject and in time, covering not only historical and literary manuscripts of medieval origin (a field in which he continued the collecting activities of Archbishop Matthew Parker) but also state papers and similar material, to the latter of which he had ready access through the proximity of his London home, Cotton House, to the repositories in the Palace of Westminster. Although it cannot be said that he had a special curiosity in heraldic manuscripts nevertheless several of great importance found their way into his library—what his friends called his 'Jewel-House'— either by individual acquisition or as items in large collections. The Camden Roll (now Cotton Roll XV. 8) of *circa* 1280 (see pp. 8–9), almost certainly reached his hands with the collections of William Camden, Clarenceux, not-withstanding the proviso in Camden's will by which, at his death in 1623, he bequeathed to Cotton, whom he described as 'the dearest of all my friends', 'all my imprinted books and manuscripts, except such as concerns arms and heraldry, the which with all my auncient seales I bequeath unto my suc-cessor in the office of Clarenceux'. Cotton certainly secured at least some part of his friend's heraldic papers (now absorbed in Cotton Faustina E. i), and some of the papers of Nicholas Charles, Lancaster, in the Cotton collec-tion may also have emanated from Camden who had bought Charles's manuscripts for £90 at the latter's death in 1613; Cotton Julius C. vii (ff. 224–228b) contains a transcript by Charles of the famous Barons' Letter to the Pope of 1301 with fine drawings of the seals attached to it. Many of the

[1] H. S. London, 'Some Mediaeval Treatises on English Heraldry', *The Antiquaries Journal*, xxxiii (1953), p. 175.

signatories to the Barons' Letter it will be recalled were present at the siege of Caerlaverock and their arms in consequence appear in the famous Caerlaverock Roll of which the earliest (and contemporary) extant copy was also in Cotton's possession (Cotton Caligula A. xviii, ff. 23b–30b) (see above p. 8 and Pl. 1). Although Camden may have been the medium through which Charles items passed into Cotton's hands, Charles was certainly himself a friend of Cotton as we can see from the few letters from Charles to Cotton (all from the last years of Charles's life) which are now in Cotton Julius C. iii (ff. 86, 87, 88). For more numerous examples of Nicholas Charles's excellent and careful work we must look in the Harleian collection, however. For the armorist, of course, far and away the most important documents in Cotton's collection are his Matthew Paris manuscript, namely, Claudius D. vi, and the single leaf inserted in Nero D. i (on both see pp. 7–8).

Of the less important fifteenth-century roll of arms known from Cotton's possession of it as the Cottonian Roll no more is necessary than the merest mention; it occupies seven leaves in Cleopatra E. viii (ff. 102–8), one of the manuscripts damaged in the 1731 fire when the library was domiciled at Ashburnham House. In Cleopatra C. iii (ff. 201b–202), a volume of church notes compiled *circa* 1583 by Francis Thynne, Lancaster, is Thynne's selection of forty-one shields in blazon from Atkinson's Roll, compiled *temp.* Henry VI and named after Edmund Atkinson, Somerset 1550–70, of which the only other (and earlier) copy is that in one of the manuscripts of William Penson, Lancaster, now in the Harleian collection (Harl. 1408). And not without elements of great heraldic interest is the spectacular manuscript, Julius E. iv, which in a series of fifty-three outline drawings presents the chief events in the life of Richard Beauchamp, Earl of Warwick (d. 1439), father-in-law of the Kingmaker; it appears to have been executed between 1485 and 1490, only a few years later than the Rous Roll, another manuscript associated with the Earls of Warwick (see pp. 25–26 below). Of its points of heraldic interest may be mentioned the investiture of the Earl as Knight of the Garter, the representation of his arms on banners and tabards, and on his helmet in the joust on f. 11b his bear and ragged-staff crest, besides portrayals of various French and English heralds, including (ff. 14–15b) the Earl's own herald. With the scene on f. 23 showing the Earl being made 'Maister' to the nine-months-old King Henry VI at his accession in 1422, should be compared that from the Rous Roll reproduced in Pl. III.

Lastly, there is evidence in an autograph memorandum by Cotton (Additional 35213, f. 33) possibly drawn up in answer to an official inquiry about the books of Sir William Dethick, Garter, that Cotton owned ten heraldic manuscripts of the arms painter and genealogist, Jacob Chaloner (1586–1631), of Chester, stepson of (and apprentice to) Randle Holme I, to whom his collections passed at his death in 1631; the memorandum is headed: 'A Catalogue of some Books Sir Robert Cotton had of on[e] Jacob Chaloner.' Chaloner certainly had interests that took him to London where he may have met Cotton, since in 1625 he petitioned for the place of Portcullis Pursuivant in the College of Arms vacant by the death of Philip Holland (see Harley

1979, f. 36b). Cotton was on friendly terms with many of the heralds, including, in addition to Camden and Charles, John Philipot, Somerset; Ralph Brooke, York; and Sir John Borough, subsequently Garter. In 1614 we find Ralph Brooke sending to Cotton in a letter now in Cotton Faustina E. i (ff. 141–142b) the results of some researches he (Brooke) had made among his own papers which showed that Clarenceux Cooke had granted 'above ·500· Coats of Armes, and that Syr Gilbert and Sr William Dethick Kings of Armes and Garters, haue geven more'. Presumably this was in answer to a query from Cotton. Why did Cotton want this information? That it came from Brooke is suspicious, since Brooke as far back as 1602 had accused Cooke of granting arms to base persons for gain and of granting to some of them arms too closely resembling those of ancient families, one of Brooke's examples it will be recalled being those granted to John Shakespeare, the poet's father. Cotton's own pride in his ancestry was notorious and is attested by the six quarterings of his armorial book-stamp. Otherwise there is little evidence of any particular interest on Cotton's part in heraldic manuscripts, though he did possess the manuscript (Nero C. iii) of Nicholas Upton's treatise 'De Studio Militari' dedicated to Humphrey, Duke of Gloucester, (see Pl. 8) which was used by Sir Edward Bysshe for his edition of Upton's work published in 1654. Perhaps we should not leave Cotton's collection without noticing the group of letters written to Cardinal Wolsey by Thomas Benolt (d. 1534), Clarenceux, and now in the three volumes in Caligula B. ii, iii, and Cleopatra C. iv, because they provide such an excellent illustration of the way in which the heralds were employed frequently in the Tudor period on diplomatic missions; both William Bruges, first Garter, and his son-in-law and successor, John Smert, besides John Writhe, third Garter, to mention no others, were all so employed (see p. 16 below).

4

Of the more notable eighteenth-century collectors other than the two Harleys whose collections passed into the possession of the Museum, Sir Hans Sloane (1660–1753), the great physician, to whom indeed the British Museum owes its foundation, appears to have had no interest in our subject and this is not surprising in view of his predominating passion for medicine and natural history; did not Pope in his Epistle to Lord Burlington write of the two great physician collectors, perhaps a little unfairly, 'And Books for Mead, and Butterflies for Sloane'? In fact among the 4,100 manuscripts in Sloane's library only one English armorial manuscript is worth noticing and that is Sloane 1301 because it contains (ff. 257–261b) a copy in blazon of the Second Dunstable Roll, now the most complete copy of the lost blazoned roll of the 135 knights present at a tournament at Dunstable in 1334; Sloane's copy was made *circa* 1590 by James Strangman, an original member of the Elizabethan Society of Antiquaries, who compiled a number of antiquarian collections relating chiefly to Essex.

5

Of the Museum's four nucleus collections of manuscripts only one remains to be mentioned and that is the Old Royal Library which owed its origin, in the main, to Edward IV. For our purpose the most important manuscript in this library, which was transferred to the Trustees of the British Museum in 1757 by George II, is that of Matthew Paris's Historia Anglorum, Royal 14 C. vii, which contains in the margins of a number of leaves no less than ninety-five painted shields of persons mentioned in the text (see also p. 7 above for other Matthew Paris manuscripts); in addition are the two reversed banners of the Hospitallers and the Templars included among the shields of the French nobles killed at Gaza in 1240, the broken shield (and sword) and the prostrate banner of William de Mareys executed in 1242 and lastly the reversed banner of France signalizing the defeat and capture of Louis IX at Mansourah in 1250. The manuscript, which is largely in Paris's own hand, may be dated to the period 1250-9. The pedigree of the Royal manuscript is well documented. Its original home was almost certainly Paris's own monastic house, St. Albans, the Abbey's press-mark appearing on folio 1 (A. 19). The manuscript subsequently belonged to Humphrey, Duke of Gloucester (d. 1447), possibly then to John Russell, Bishop of Lincoln (d. 1494), later to Henry Fitzalan, Earl of Arundel (d. 1580) (who lent it to Archbishop Parker for the latter's edition of the Chronica published in 1571), next to his son-in-law, John, Lord Lumley (d. 1609), and went thence to the Royal Library by the purchase of Lumley's library at his death by James I for Henry, Prince of Wales. Few manuscripts have had a more interesting and distinguished pedigree—or more notable users: Polydore Vergil, the historian, used it during his stay in England from 1502 to 1550 and left many autograph notes in it, and it was seen by the antiquary and controversialist, John Bale, in the Royal Library between 1549 and 1559; indeed the acquisition of the manuscript by the Earl of Arundel may have been made possible by its having been perhaps in Bale's hands as a borrowing from the Royal Library. Armorially it is of course a most precious document and its collection of painted shields makes it our earliest extant roll of arms, an example, strictly speaking, of an Illustrative Roll. It has, too, the added value so far as Matthew Paris is concerned of showing us the lively interest he took in heraldry, which is not surprising considering that in his time heraldry was a part of everyday life. It has been happily said by the late Mr. Tremlett, the editor of the Paris shields in Aspilogia II, that 'Matthew learnt his heraldry as he learnt the events he chronicled'.

6

Of the two greatest seventeenth-century heralds, Elias Ashmole and Sir William Dugdale, the Museum possesses only stray items from their collections since in both cases these have found a permanent home elsewhere (the Bodleian Library at Oxford); however, the former's signature appears in the Oldhall Hours discussed below (see p. 20), and another manuscript almost certainly at one time in Ashmole's possession is one of the most important heraldic volumes in the Department. This is the manuscript entitled Bruges' Garter Book, from which figures of the first Founder Knights of the Garter, while the book was in Ashmole's hands, were etched by Wenceslaus Hollar for Ashmole's great work entitled *The Institution of the Order of the Garter* published in 1672. Subsequently, it was acquired by one of the greatest of all the Garter Kings of Arms, John Anstis the Elder (d. 1744), who told Francis Peck, the historian of Stamford, that he had bought it for five guineas. Among its later owners was John Towneley (d. 1813), the heir and uncle of Charles Towneley, the famous collector of classical antiquities, and the owner of the Towneley Homer, a notable Greek manuscript later in the library of Fanny Burney's brother, Dr. Charles Burney. At Towneley's sale Bruges' Book was bought by Richard Grenville, first Duke of Buckingham and Chandos, and housed by him with the rest of his library at Stowe in Buckinghamshire. After many vicissitudes the Stowe manuscripts were acquired by the British Museum in 1883 and Bruges' Garter Book then received its present pressmark, Stowe 594. The presence in it of annotations by John Writhe, third Garter 1478–1504, and the fact that at least one of the secondary shields (which were painted at different times by different hands) is the work of one of Sir Thomas Wriothesley's artists (see above, p. 11) suggested to Mr. Stanford London that the book may have passed from Garter to Garter perhaps down to Sir William Dethick who resigned the Gartership in 1606 and died in 1612. This magnificent manuscript, measuring $11\frac{1}{4} \times 15$ inches, contains no less than twenty-six full-page coloured drawings of the Founder Knights of the Garter, of Edward III and of Garter King of Arms kneeling before St. George, and is the earliest known armorial of the Order of the Garter; the kneeling figure is Bruges himself, first Garter and the originator of the manuscript. Besides being the earliest known armorial of the Order it is important also heraldically as being perhaps the prototype of the whole class of 'Visitations with men of arms' such as the pictorial visitations of Roger Legh, Le Neve's Equestrian Roll and the Salisbury Roll; a foreign example is the equestrian armorial of the Toison d'Or. Bruges, who died in 1450, was a most interesting man and fully deserved the full-scale biography devoted to him by Mr. Hugh Stanford London, Norfolk Herald Extraordinary, published posthumously in 1970. His father, Richard Bruges, had been Lancaster Herald to John of Gaunt, Duke of Lancaster, from possibly as early as 1380, and retained the title under Henry IV, on whose accession (1399) he was made King of Arms of the Northern Province. He was one of the heralds often employed on missions abroad. In this respect our present subject, William Bruges, followed his father's example for he too was a herald who specialized in diplomatic work; indeed under Henry VI hardly a year passed in which he was not sent on at least one foreign mission. The paintings in his Garter Book were made probably about 1430, a date indicated by a possible connection with the Duke of Burgundy's institution of the office of Toison d'Or King of Arms in November 1431, the first holder of that office being Jean Lefèvre sieur de Saint Rémy who was almost certainly

I. Military Roll. Knights jousting. Before 1448

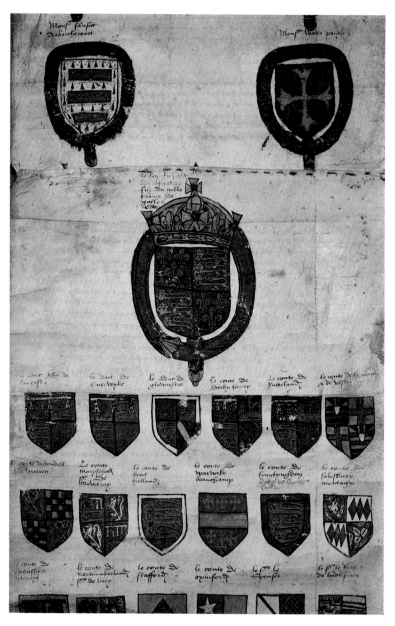

II. Willement's Roll. Gartered and crowned shield of arms of Richard II, compiled 1392–7.
Early sixteenth-century *copy*

associated with Bruges as a result of the latter's frequent visits to Flanders, notably those in 1429 and 1431. St. Rémy too was responsible for the Golden Fleece equestrian armorial referred to above and it is not without significance in this connection that art historians have seen in the paintings in Bruges' Garter Book strong Flemish influence. At his death in 1450 Bruges was buried in St. George's, Stamford, to which he was a great benefactor, giving large sums for its rebuilding and, what is of particular interest to us at this point, providing for the glazing of the windows with figures of Edward III and the Founder Knights of the Garter, painted glass which remained more or less intact until its destruction in the 1730s when the lamentable story of what happened is recorded in his diary by William Stukeley, the antiquary, at that time Rector of All Saints, Stamford. The Bruges family heraldic tradition was continued in the person of William's successor in the Gartership, John Smert, who married William Bruges' daughter and heir, Katherine.

But although this is the most important of the heraldic manuscripts in the Stowe collection there are many others, of which Stowe 696 is of special note being the sixteenth-century copy in trick and blazon of the collection of arms commonly designated Thomas Jenyns' Book, a copy made when the original was in the hands of Robert Glover, Somerset, in 1578, as we learn from the memorandum on folio 1 signed both by Glover himself and William Flower, Norroy King of Arms. This is a very large collection of coats, the nucleus possibly being Cooke's or Cotgrave's Ordinary of *circa* 1340 according to Sir Anthony Wagner. Of the copy with painted shields known as Queen Margaret's Version, dating from about 1473 perhaps (Additional 40851), something has been said above (see p. 9 and Pl. 5).

Apart from these individual items in the Stowe collection most important heraldically is the large group of manuscripts that had formerly belonged to John Anstis the Elder, Garter until his death at Mortlake in 1744, who has been described as one of the most learned members of the College. His manuscripts passed at his death, first, to his son John Anstis the younger and then on the latter's death in 1754 to his brother the Reverend George Anstis; on the death of the last named they were sold by auction in 1768. At the sale many Anstis manuscripts were acquired by Thomas Astle (1735–1803), the antiquary (son-in-law of the Essex historian Philip Morant), Keeper of the Records in the Tower, and perhaps best known today as the author of *The Origin and Progress of Writing*, first published in 1784. Under the terms of his will Astle's manuscripts were acquired for the nominal sum of £500 by the Duke of Buckingham and in this way some, but by no means all, of the Anstis manuscripts reached their present home in the Stowe collection in the British Museum; there is no evidence, for example, that Astle ever owned Bruges' Garter Book. Of volumes other than those containing collections compiled by him, Anstis seems to have owned somewhat more than a dozen of those that now bear Stowe press-marks. Of these, one (Stowe 692), an alphabet of arms, had belonged to an early Garter, Sir Christopher Barker, Garter 1536–49, and two (Stowe 440 and 580) had been in the possession of a more recent predecessor in the Gartership, Sir

Edward Walker (d. 1677), and bear on their covers Walker's armorial book-stamp; another (Stowe 601) had belonged at one time to Henry Chitting, (d. 1638), Chester Herald, and is bound in the limp vellum binding bearing his coat of arms characteristic of his books, of which several examples are preserved in the Harleian collection; a fifth Anstis volume that had at one time been in the hands of a herald is the little commonplace book (Stowe 1047) compiled by Francis Thynne (d. 1608), Lancaster, which contains extracts by him from English chronicles, monastic records, etc. Of greater importance than Thynne's commonplace book, however, is that of Francis Tate (Stowe 1045), which is of immense value for the history of the Elizabethan Society of Antiquaries, containing as it does notes of the subjects (many of heraldic interest) proposed for discussion at the society's various meetings, with the names of the members present and the dates of the meetings. There is no evidence that this was an Anstis volume, nor does he appear to have owned the book of heraldic collections (Stowe 668) that had belonged to Robert Glover, Somerset, who died in the Armada year. Of the many volumes of Anstis's own compilation in the Stowe collection special mention should be made of his uncompleted and unpublished treatise on heraldic seals preserved in two volumes (Stowe 665, 666) and entitled 'Aspilogia, sive de Iconibus scutariis gentilitiis commentarius'. These two Stowe manuscripts were among those owned by Astle, who made additions to them and whose armorial bookstamp appears on the covers. The title was appropriated by Anstis from that given by Sir Henry Spelman to his treatise on heraldry published posthumously in 1654; it is now perpetuated as the title of the series of volumes of heraldic material at present in process of joint publication by the Society of Antiquaries and the Harleian Society. Among the several other Stowe volumes of Anstis's own compilation is one of particular interest to Anstis's biographer, namely, Stowe 633, which contains, in addition to a genealogy of the Anstis family, a brief autobiography of Anstis himself from his own pen, which may be read with not a little interest beside the vivid portrait of him sketched in some detail by his younger colleague in the College of Arms and a subsequent Garter, Stephen Martin Leake, which has been printed by Sir Anthony Wagner in his *Heralds of England*, 1967 (pp. 320–3) from the College of Arms manuscript in which it is preserved. Anstis's name should at any rate be mentioned in this book with honour since he was a generous donor to the manuscript portion of the Harleian Library (discussed above, pp. 10–12), presenting to its founder, Robert Harley, 1st Earl of Oxford, no less than forty-four manuscripts, his nearest rival in this respect being Peter Le Neve, Norroy. Anstis's gifts of these manuscripts (mostly in 1719, in addition to a number of charters in 1716) bore dividends as is shown by a remark made by Humfrey Wanley in a letter to Anstis written in 1725 (Stowe 749, f. 256) that 'my lord' [Edward Harley] had said 'you had been a Benefactor to the Library, & therefore may command anything that he hath', and Anstis makes frequent appearances in the pages of Wanley's diary, as does another herald, and one of a much less pleasant character, John Warburton, Somerset, who was described by a colleague as 'another Ralph Brooke, but a much worse man and not so good a herald'. Had Wanley been successful one of the more important of Warburton's heraldic manuscripts would have a place today in the Harleian collection, but although Warburton did in fact sell to Harley a number of manuscripts (not a few of great interest and many at one time in the library at Naworth having belonged to Lord William Howard), after a vain all-night tavern 'frolic' intended by Warburton to 'Muddle' Wanley and so gain an increase in price, he would not part with the desired item; Warburton in an 'angry' reply, records Wanley in his diary under 6 October 1720, 'falsely affirming that the Heraldical MS. I desired him to add to the Parcel he designed to sell my Lord [Harley] bring's him in half his Livelyhood'. The volume in question would seem to be the Baronagium Genealogicum, a collection of pedigrees of the families of peers said to have been started by Sir William Segar, Garter, and continued by his great-grandson, Simon Segar; this book, however, remained in Warburton's hands and appeared in the sale of his manuscripts in 1759.[1] Warburton's Yorkshire collections have, however, found a place in the Department coming into the Museum's possession with the purchase in 1807 of the great mass of manuscripts brought together by William Petty, 1st Marquess of Lansdowne; they contain some heraldic material here and there and are now Lansdowne 886–99, 908–18, and 923. The heraldic and armorial collections of several other heralds are represented by single items in this (the Lansdowne) collection; mention may be made of Sir William Segar's Book of Funerals begun *circa* 1600 (Lansdowne 872); Richard Leigh's Visitation of Oxfordshire taken by him as Portcullis Pursuivant in 1574 as Deputy to Clarenceux Cooke (Lansdowne 880); and Sir William Dugdale's notes of the arms recorded on his 1663 and 1664 Staffordshire Visitations (Lansdowne 857). And a mass of heraldic and other material in Lansdowne 860 A, B, partly by Henry Ferrers (1594–1633) of Baddesley Clinton introduces us to a little-known Warwickshire antiquary whose person has recently been given life in a Dugdale Society paper by Miss Elizabeth Berry; Ferrers was also (according to the Lansdowne Catalogue) the donor of Lansdowne 861 to Sir Richard St. George, Clarenceux, some volumes of whose heraldic collections also found their way into the Lansdowne collection.

7

Although not heraldic in their *contents* there are, of course, many other manuscripts in the collections that are of interest to the student of heraldry; I refer to those manuscripts, many of medieval date, which contain, usually on their first leaves, painted coats of arms of their previous owners. In one collection not so far referred to, that portion of the manuscript assemblage formed mostly by Thomas Howard, 2nd Earl of Arundel, who died at Padua in 1646, which was transferred to the British Museum from the Royal Society in 1831, are several volumes adorned with such painted coats of arms.

[1] It is now in the College of Arms, having been acquired by the College in 1860.

In Arundel 74, a fourteenth-century manuscript of Bede's Ecclesiastical History, occurs the painted coat of Henry le Despenser, Bishop of Norwich 1370–1407, the fighting bishop who defeated the Norfolk rebels in the 1381 rising, other examples of whose armorial insignia are to be found on several leaves in Cotton Claudius E. viii. Sir Robert Cotton, indeed, had his own coat of arms painted in one manuscript, Claudius D. ii, a fourteenth- and fifteenth-century manuscript of Statuta Anglie to which, strictly speaking, he had no title at all, the manuscript belonging to the Corporation of the City of London having been at one time in the Guildhall. Another example of the way in which Cotton had his arms painted in a manuscript is Cotton Nero A. ii, a 'uolumen . . . fragmentorum' as he called it, the first leaf of which is a detached page from a late fifteenth-century Flemish illuminated manuscript inserted in his 'uolumen' as a decorative frontispiece and adorned with his painted shield of arms (reproduced in F. Wormald and C. E. Wright, *The English Library*, 1958, Pl. 16). To return to the Arundel manuscripts it will suffice in this connection to mention the breviary in Arundel 130 which bears the coat of arms of Henry Percy, 3rd Earl of Northumberland, who owned the book between 1446 and 1461; the manuscript of Lydgate's poem on the Siege and Destruction of Thebes, Arundel 119, which was written for Geoffrey Chaucer's grandson-in-law, the much hated and ill-fated William de la Pole, 1st Duke of Suffolk, beheaded at sea off Dover in 1450, and bears his arms quartering Wingfield on folio 4; and the arms of Margaret of York, Duchess of Burgundy, sister of Edward IV, appear on the richly illuminated leaf from a gradual in Arundel 71 (f. 9), believed at one time to have belonged to a book given by her to the Grey Friars at Greenwich; while several Arundel manuscripts (366, 435, 454, 461) bear the arms of Cardinal John Morton, Archbishop of Canterbury (d. 1500), today remembered, notoriously, as the originator of 'Morton's Fork' and, more kindly, as the builder of 'Morton's Dyke' in the Fens. Of more particular interest to the armorist are the arms of Thomas Wall, Garter 1534, that are painted on folio 103b in a manuscript of Occleve's poem, De Regimine Principum, Arundel 59, which he purchased while Windsor Herald in 1528, since these, the Wall arms, as borne by Thomas, Garter, and his son, Thomas, Norroy, have been the subject of some discussion by armorists.

8

Manuscripts enriched with the arms of their former owners are to be found, of course, in all the Department's collections and are so numerous that only a few further examples can be added to those cited above. The Oldhall Hours, Harley 2900, bears on folio 55 the arms of Sir William Oldhall of Narford, and on folio 200 those of his wife, Margaret, daughter of William, 5th Baron Willoughby of Eresby (the two coats impaled are also painted on the fore-edge of the manuscript). Harley 2639 bears (f. 2) the arms of John Tiptoft, Earl of Worcester (executed in 1470), and Harley 1197 (f. 402) the coat of arms (roughly painted) of Cardinal Wolsey, while Harley 3862 is adorned on its first leaf with the painted coat of John de Vere, 13th Earl of Oxford (d. 1513). The Royal manuscripts are, as one would expect, rich in instances of royal coats, one of the best known being that of Henry VII since it appears in the famous and oft-reproduced picture of the White Tower in the Tower of London in Royal 16 F. ii; and that of Henry VIII is embroidered on the red velvet binding that clothes Royal 20 A. iv (an exceptionally beautiful example of the Department's rich collection of armorial bindings, to which there is no room for more than this passing reference); and Royal 18 A. xii bears on folio 49 the arms of Anne Neville, wife of Richard III. Of more interest to the historian of the heralds, however, will be (in addition to the Wall coat referred to above) the bull's head crest of Sir Thomas Wriothesley, Garter (d. 1534), at the foot of folio 2 in Lansdowne 285, the painted coat of Sir William Dethick, Garter (d. 1612), in Harley 1864 (f. 1b), and that of Sir William Le Neve, York Herald (d. 1661), (with his signatures, twice) in the margin of folio 1 of Royal 17 D. xx (see Pl. 15), and the fine example of the armorial bookstamp of John Philipot, Somerset (d. 1645), on Harley 5829.

9

The heraldic material so far discussed (pp. 10–20 above) has been drawn either from the four nucleus collections—Sloane, Cotton, Harley, and Royal—or from such subsequent large block acquisitions as the Stowe, Lansdowne, and Arundel. Since the formation of the Museum in 1753, however, manuscripts have been continuously acquired and incorporated in a vast series to which has been assigned the title 'Additional' or, in the case of those purchased from a special fund, 'Egerton', and since the Museum's foundation successive Keepers of Manuscripts have taken the opportunity of increasing, *inter alia*, the holdings of heraldic manuscripts as occasion has offered, as witness the purchase of the English version of the Rous Roll in 1955 (see pp. 10, 25–26 and Pl. III) and Willement's Roll in the preceding year (see pp. 9, 24 and Pl. II).

Most of the heraldic manuscripts so acquired have been obtained for the most part through the dispersal of three kinds of libraries, usually, but by no means always, by auction, namely: (i) libraries and collections formed by heralds themselves and dispersed at death, examples of which are those of Sir George Nayler, Garter, in 1832 and Sir George Young, Garter, in 1871; (ii) material brought together by antiquaries and collectors with strong heraldic interests, such as the Reverend John Newling, Prebendary of Lichfield (d. 1838), part of whose collections was acquired by a nobleman with similar interests, William Noel-Hill, 3rd Baron Berwick of Attingham, who died in 1842, and Evelyn Philip Shirley of Ettington Park in Warwickshire (d. 1882), the 'Mr. Ardenne' of Disraeli's *Lothair* (1870), who owned the fifteenth-century Shirley Roll and whose library remained intact until its dispersal at Sotheby's in 1947, and who is still well known as the author of

The Noble and Gentle Men of England, first published in 1859; and (iii) large family libraries such as that of the Dukes of Hamilton sold in 1882 and 1883 or the Clumber Library of the Dukes of Newcastle so named after their Nottinghamshire seat and dispersed at Sotheby's in 1958, not to mention the vast accumulation of manuscripts of all kinds made by that omniverous collector Sir Thomas Phillipps, housed first at Middle Hill and later at Thirlestaine House at Cheltenham, and dispersed in a number of sales from 1886 onwards.

10

From all of these sources have been derived additions to the Department's heraldic collections. Thus, from the library of Sir George Nayler (d. 1831) came important additions to the Department's holdings of John Anstis material, which include, for example, collections by him relating to the Court of Chivalry (Additional 9021–2), heralds' duties (Additional 9016), fees (Additional 9019), funerals, grants of arms and duels (Additional 9018), and ceremonies (Additional 9017). Nayler also owned at least three important heraldic manuscripts acquired by the Museum in the present century, namely, Sir Thomas Wriothesley's volume of painted drawings of standards which includes also his copy (in trick) of part of the Fenwick Roll (Fenwick A) (Additional 45132), Sir Thomas Holme's Book II (Additional 45133), and Writhe's Book of Knights (Additional 46354), of which the first two came through the Clumber Sale and the last from the 1946 Phillipps sale (see below, p. 25). From Nayler's library also (but in 1858, long after his sale) came the fourteen volumes (Additional 22292–305) containing impressions taken from the armorial coffin-plates of the English nobility and gentry from 1727 to 1831.

11

The Museum's purchases at the sales of several heralds' libraries, however, contain very little of heraldic interest. At those in 1854 and 1860 of that of Sir William Betham (d. 1853), Ulster King of Arms 1820, the Museum obtained directly at the sales many manuscripts (Additional 19828–65, 23683–7, etc.), but hardly any to our present purpose. As most of his collections were bequeathed to the College of Arms, this is inevitably true also of the sale in 1871 of the residue of the Library of Sir George Young (d. 1861), Garter 1842, said to be the original of 'Sir Vavasour Firebrace' in Disraeli's *Sybil* (1845); Additional 28842–53 belonged to Young, while letters from him to numerous correspondents (including especially Sir Frederic Madden and the Reverend Philip Bliss, the antiquary) are widely scattered in the later Additionals.

Quite otherwise, however, is the case of two recent acquisitions by the Museum. In 1951 the Trustees of Lucy, Countess of Egmont (d. 1912), presented the archive known as the Egmont Papers (Additional 46920–47213). A very large part of this archive consists of the Perceval family papers, but John Perceval, 1st Earl of Egmont (1753), had a passion for genealogy and especially the history of his own family, a passion which he was to develop more strongly after his withdrawal from politics following a clash with Walpole and which inspired in him a more general interest in heraldic matters; as a result he acquired many volumes from the papers of the St. George family and the St. George portion of the archive (Additional 47171–89, 47195) includes three heraldic and genealogical manuscripts of Nicholas Charles, Lancaster, Additional 47177–9, three similar volumes by Henry Lilly, Rouge Dragon Pursuivant, Additional 47185–7, and a notebook compiled by Gregory King, Lancaster, during the visitation of Cambridgeshire and Huntingdonshire when as Rouge Dragon he accompanied Sir Henry St. George the younger, Clarenceux, Additional 47189; a transcript by George Harbin of a genealogical history of the house of Carew compiled by John Anstis (Additional 47192) and another by James Green, Bluemantle (who had been clerk successively to the Garters Sir Henry St. George the Younger and John Anstis), of Robert Dale's transcript of the 1690 catalogue of the College of Arms library (Additional 47193), of which a copy was already in the Department's collections in Lansdowne 689. Lastly, mention should be made of the one medieval manuscript item in the Egmont Papers, a roll-genealogy of the kings of England (Additional 47170), which claims to be the work of Walter of Whittlesey, the monk of Peterborough whose chronicle and cartulary of Peterborough Abbey, Additional 39758, contains the Peterborough Roll (see p. 8 and Pl. 2).

Two years later (1953) the Department's heraldic collections received a notable addition in the papers of Stephen Martin Leake (d. 1775), Garter 1754, summarily characterized by Garter Young as an 'Ornament to the College', to which additions had been made by his son, John (d. 1836; Chester Herald 1752–91); the major part of Leake's heraldic collections (seventy-five volumes) was acquired by the College of Arms in 1834 from the executor of his son George (Chester Herald 1791–1834). The heraldic material in the Martin Leake collection is comprised in Additional 47979–83; a small group of manuscripts in the collection bear witness also to his numismatic interests (Additional 47990–3).

Generally speaking, of course, the heralds' own collections have found their way (in part at least if not as a whole) into the College of Arms (as we have seen in the case of Sir George Young and Stephen Martin Leake) and it is on the opportunities afforded by the dispersal of the collections or libraries in the second and third categories described above (pp. 21–22) that the Museum has been most dependent for the heraldic manuscripts that have come into its possession since 1753. Thus, Volume II of the Furness Coucher Book (Additional 33244) (Volume I still remains in the Duchy of Lancaster records in the Public Record Office), written by John Stell in 1412 for Abbot W. de Dalton, which contains fifty-one shields of the arms of the benefactors to Furness Abbey, painted in the initials of the copies in it of the Abbey's charters, and is thus an excellent example (like the Peterborough Roll) of an 'Illustrative Roll', was acquired by the Museum in 1886 from Dr. Lippmann of Berlin, being one of the items bought by the Prussian Government at the Hamilton sale in 1882, having been in the hands of the Dukes of Hamilton apparently from 1796 until that year; it was still in the Duchy of Lancaster Office in 1735 but shortly afterwards was in the possession of the elusive collector Ralph Palmer. The Peterborough Roll (Additional 39758) (see p. 8 and Pl. 2) was bought at Sotheby's in 1918 at the sale of books from the Fitzwilliam library at Milton Hall, near Peterborough, its first Fitzwilliam owner having been possibly William, the 1st Earl Fitzwilliam, who died in 1722, and an 'Occasional Roll', the Boroughbridge Roll (Egerton 2850), which contains on its dorse the names and blazoned shields of those involved in the battle of Boroughbridge fought in 1322 as a result of the rebellion of Thomas, Earl of Lancaster, had been acquired in 1903 having been for many years in the possession of the Williams Wynn family of Coed-y-Maen. In 1923 the Museum secured at Sotheby's Sir John Fenn's Book of Badges (Additional 40742), compiled *circa* 1466–70 and containing fifty-seven badges, mainly of Yorkist nobles, drawn boldly in ink and painted, which derives its name from its one-time owner Sir John Fenn (d. 1794), the possessor and first editor of the famous Paston letters (once, it may be observed in passing, in the possession of Peter Le Neve, Norroy); among the badges may be instanced the falcon and fetterlock of the Duke of York (f. 5), the chained bear of the Earls of Warwick (f. 10), the white hind of Joan, the Fair Maid of Kent (f. 6), and the white lion of the Earl of March (f. 8).

15

From the notable heraldic library of the Reverend John Newling (see p. 21), who died at Lichfield in 1838, derives Willement's Roll so called from its first editor, Thomas Willement (d. 1871), the heraldic antiquary and stained-glass artist, who published it in blazon in 1834; after Newling's death it disappeared from view, not to reappear until 24 March 1954 when it came on to the market as lot 252 in the sale at Christie's of books from the library of Lord Derby (now Egerton 3713); the roll, a general one, containing in its present form some 600 shields, is a late fifteenth- or early sixteenth-century copy of a roll originally compiled between 1392 and 1397 (see pp. 9, 25

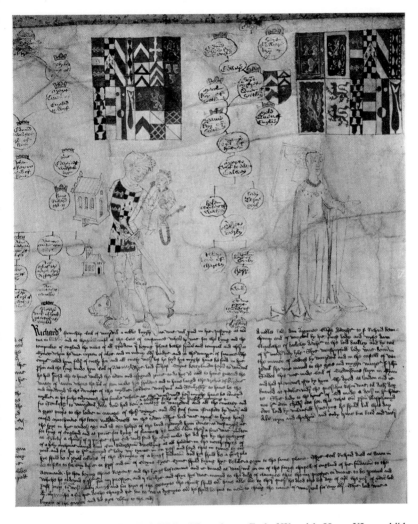

III. Rous Roll (English Version). Richard Beauchamp, Earl of Warwick, Henry VI as a child, and the Earl's daughter, Margaret, wife of John Talbot, Earl of Shrewsbury. *Temp*. Richard III

IV. Collections relating to standards and banners made between 1525 and 1554 for Sir Thomas Wriothesley, Garter King of Arms 1505–34

and Pl. II). Another clerical heraldic enthusiast was the Reverend David Thomas Powell (d. 1848) who, after serving in Flanders as a lieutenant in the 14th Light Dragoons, entered Magdalen College in 1798: his library was sold in 1848 and various manuscripts in it began then a series of travels, those of two of which ended in the British Museum with the acquisition in 1912 of Additional 38537, a copy of the Dering Roll which had belonged in 1597 to the antiquary Ralph Starkey and *circa* 1640 to Sir Edward Dering, 1st Bart., the politician and antiquary, great-grandfather to the 1st Earl of Egmont whose collections have been described above (see p. 23), and in 1865 of Additional 26677, Powell's own *facsimile copy*, made in 1812, of the Roll now known after him as Powell's Roll, a book painted with 672 shields executed *circa* 1350 and now in the Bodleian Library at Oxford (Ashmole 804. IV).

16

Among the original rolls acquired, two may be mentioned here, namely, the [Third] Calais Roll of *circa* 1348 was acquired in 1875 and is now Additional 29502 (for description see p. 8 above) and the Parliament Roll of 1515, a roll of the lords spiritual and temporal, with arms in colour (published by Thomas Willement in facsimile in 1829), was acquired in 1921 and is now Additional 40078. The Museum is fortunate also in possessing in the reproduction of Writhe's Garter Armorial, Additional 37340, acquired in 1906, an example of the series of Hatton–Dugdale facsimiles made *circa* 1640 for Sir Christopher Hatton probably by the arms-painter William Sedgwick under the direction of Sir William Dugdale and possibly at Kirby Hall, Hatton's house in Northamptonshire (see Pl. 11). Of all the recent acquisitions of heraldic manuscripts, however, the most important is the group associated with the studio of Sir Thomas Wriothesley (d. 1534), Garter (see p. 10), namely, Additional 45131, collections relating to funerals, Additional 45132, a volume made up mostly of painted drawings of banners (see Pl. IV) but including Wriothesley's copy of the Fenwick roll (ff. 92b–95b, 137–149b), and Additional 45133, Sir Thomas Holme's Book II, comprising copies of the Parliamentary and other rolls (see Pll. IV, 12, 13), all three of which were acquired, as noted above (p. 22) at the Clumber sale in 1938 and were formerly in Sir George Nayler's possession; to which may be added Writhe's Book of Knights, Additional 46354, acquired in 1946.

17

If the Museum was lucky enough to secure a 'lost' roll of arms in 1954 with the acquisition of Willement's Roll at Christie's, it had the still greater good fortune to purchase by negotiation in the following year another and much more famous 'lost' roll, nothing less splendid than the manuscript of the English and 'Yorkist' version of the Rous Roll (now Additional 48976), one of the two armorial roll-chronicles executed by John Rous (d. 1491), chantry priest at Guy's Cliffe, to celebrate the fame and exploits of the Beauchamp and Neville Earls of Warwick his patrons; it was seen by Horace Walpole in 1768, published in facsimile by William Courthope, Somerset Herald, in 1859, and last recorded in 1869 among the Duke of Manchester's manuscripts at Kimbolton Castle (see Pl. III). The roll, some 24 feet in length and 13½ inches in height, contains no less than sixty-four portraits of the royal and other benefactors of Warwick and of holders of the Warwick earldom, all executed delicately in pen and ink with their painted coats of arms (most of them bannerwise) over their heads. Many figures are accompanied by their badges and each has below, in English, a brief biographical notice. The roll must have been made between 1483 and 1485, the last figures on it being those of Richard III, his wife Anne Neville, the younger daughter of the Kingmaker, Richard Neville, Earl of Warwick, and their son Edward, Prince of Wales; in this version of the roll the queen is regally habited, holding in her right hand the sceptre, while both Richard and his son wear royal crowns. The death of Richard on Bosworth Field in 1485 and the death of his queen in the same year destroyed the Yorkist cause and the fortunes of the Nevilles (Edward having died in 1484), and thus rendered the possession of a roll so Yorkist in flavour inexpedient, to say the least. In the second (and Latin) version of his two roll-chronicles, that now in the College of Arms (which in 1640 was still the owner also of the English version), Rous therefore substituted a 'Lancastrian' colouring, one obviously more acceptable to the new Tudor King, Henry VII, who had become head of the house of Lancaster in 1471; among other changes, Anne is deprived of her regal habit and the figure of Edward of Westminster, Henry VI's son and Anne's first husband, who had died in 1471, is inserted. On the verso of the Museum roll are ninety-four painted coats of arms against each of which is inscribed (twice) the name of the holder and, most important of all, the following inscription in large Gothic letters contemporary with the text of the roll: 'This rol was laburd and finished by Master John Rows of Warrewyk.' The Rous Roll, of course, is also a precious specimen of fifteenth-century English art and perhaps here, to conclude, it may not be out of place to refer to the magnificent example of East Anglian illumination, the Luttrell Psalter (Additional 45130), since no one, heraldically minded or otherwise, can be ignorant of the splendid illumination on folio 202b showing with a wealth of heraldry the Lincolnshire knight bachelor, Sir Geoffrey Luttrell of Irnham (d. 1345), for whom the manuscript was executed ('Dominus Galfridus Louterell me fieri fecit' wrote the scribe above the miniature itself), seated in armour on horseback, the Luttrell arms (*az*, a bend between six martlets *arg*) depicted on his shield, his surcoat and the fan-crest of his helmet, on the trapper of his horse and the pennon of his lance; standing beside him are his wife, Agnes Sutton, wearing a gown of the Luttrell arms impaling those of Sutton (*or*, a lion rampant *vert*) who is handing to him his gilded helm and holding his pennoned lance, and his daughter-in-law, Beatrice Scrope, wife of his son and heir Sir Andrew Luttrell, wearing a gown of the Luttrell arms impaling those of Scrope of Masham (*az* a bend *or*, differenced by a label of five points *arg* of which only three are visible),

26

who is holding his shield (see the coloured frontispiece to the British Museum facsimile published in 1952). Here brought vividly before us is the part heraldry played in everyday life in the Middle Ages.

18

Lastly to what has been said above it will suffice to observe by way of conclusion that the additions made over the past two centuries to the Department's heraldic manuscripts have included also such beautifully executed pedigrees as that of the family of Hesketh of Rufford (adorned with painted portraits and coats of arms), executed for the family *circa* 1594 (acquired in 1935, Additional 44026), the Lyte pedigree tracing the descent of King James I from Brutus, compiled between 1605 and 1610 (acquired in 1954, Additional 48343), and Sir William Segar's pedigree of the Westons of Sutton Place in Surrey drawn up in 1632 and described by J. Horace Round, that fearsome critic of the heralds, as 'a little concoction of his own' (acquired in 1881, Additional 31890); such first-class examples of Church Notes as William Burton's of Leicestershire (Egerton 3510) and John Philipot's of Kent (Egerton 3310 A; see Pl. 16); such original grants of arms as those made in the years 1467 to 1556 and brought together in Additional 37687 or that of Robert Cooke, Clarenceux, to Matthew Parker's son in 1572 (Egerton 2581B) or that to Sir Nicholas Bacon (Additional 39249), reproduced in Pl. 14, to select no others, besides such collections made by the lesser-known heralds like William Colbarne, Laurence Dalton, Thomas Hawley (who as Rouge Croix took to James IV of Scotland the English challenge to Flodden Field and brought back to Henry VIII the news of the battle), and William Wyrley, and others too numerous to mention in a short survey of this kind.

Select Bibliography

Brault, Gerard J., *Early Blazon. Heraldic Terminology in the 12th and 13th Centuries*, Oxford, 1972.

College of Arms, The, by Walter Hindes Godfrey, Anthony Richard Wagner, and Hugh Stanford London, London Survey Committee, vol. xvi, 1963.

Denholm-Young, N. *History and Heraldry 1254 to 1310. A Study of the Historical Value of the Rolls of Arms*, Oxford, 1965.

Hope, W. H. St. John, *A Grammar of English Heraldry*, 2nd edn., revised by Sir Anthony R. Wagner, Cambridge, 1953.

Hope, W. H. St. John, *Heraldry for Craftsmen and Designers*, 1929.

London, Hugh Stanford, *Royal Beasts*, The Heraldry Society, 1956.

London, Hugh Stanford, 'Willement's Roll', *The Coat of Arms*, vol. iv, no. 28 (Oct. 1956), pp. 153–4.

London, Hugh Stanford, *The Life of William Bruges, the first Garter King of Arms*, The Harleian Society, vols. 111 and 112, 1970.

Rolls of Arms Henry III. The Matthew Paris Shields, ed. T. D. Tremlett and Glover's Roll and Walford's Roll, ed. H. S. London, with additions and corrections to *A Catalogue of English Mediaeval Rolls of Arms* by Sir Anthony Wagner, The Society of Antiquaries, Aspilogia II, and The Harleian Society, vols. 113 and 114, 1967.

Scott-Giles, C. Wilfrid, *The Romance of Heraldry*, 1929; revised edn., 1965.

Wagner, Sir Anthony Richard, *Heraldry in England*, King Penguin, 1946.

Wagner, Sir Anthony Richard, *A Catalogue of British Mediaeval Rolls of Arms*, The Society of Antiquaries, Aspilogia I, and The Harleian Society, vol. 100, 1950.

Wagner, Sir Anthony Richard, *The Records and Collections of the College of Arms*, Burke's Peerage, 1952.

Wagner, Sir Anthony Richard, *Heralds and Heraldry in the Middle Ages. An Inquiry into the Growth of the Armorial Function of Heralds*, 1939; 2nd edn., 1956.

Wagner, Sir Anthony Richard, *Heralds of England. A History of the Office and College of Arms*, 1967.

Wright, Cyril Ernest, 'Willement's Roll', *British Museum Quarterly*, vol. xix (1954), p. 49, pl. XVII.

Wright, Cyril Ernest, 'The Rous Roll', *British Museum Quarterly*, vol. xx (1955–6), pp. 77–81, pl. XXVI.

Wright, Cyril Ernest, *Fontes Harleiani. A Study of the Sources of the Harleian Collection of Manuscripts preserved in the Department of Manuscripts in the British Museum*, 1972.

Glossary of terms used in the Text

Arg   argent, silver.

Az   azure, blue.

Banner   a rectangular flag, in medieval times having the longer side upright, decorated with the bearer's coat of arms.

Barry   having a number of bands or bars.

Bend   a band running diagonally from the corner of the shield.

Blazon   to describe the field, charges, etc., of a coat of arms in correct heraldic language.

Crest   a device (such as a lion, for example) fixed upon the helm.

Double-queued   descriptive of an animal with two tails.

Ermine   a conventional representation of the fur.

Gorged   an animal is said to be gorged, when a coronet or crown is shown round its neck.

Gu   gules, red.

Guidon   resembles in form the standard (see below) but ends in a point.

Impaled   a method of setting two coats of arms on a shield side by side, used, for example, for displaying the arms of man and wife.

Mantling   a scarf or cloth hanging over the helm.

Or   gold.

Ordinary (of arms)   a roll of arms on which the latter are grouped by the charges (for example, lions, eagles) and not by the holders of the arms.

Passant   descriptive of animals walking.

Pennon   resembles the standard in form and is half the size of the guidon (see above) and bears only arms.

Rampant   descriptive of animals when in an erect position.

Standard   an elongated flag split at the ends, containing Cross of St. George (by the staff), and the bearer's motto, crest, and badge, but never the arms.

Tabard   a short loose outer garment worn over armour or by heralds.

Torse   a twisted wreath or bandeau of two or more differently coloured stuffs masking the junction of the crest with the helm.

Trick   to indicate on an outline sketch of a shield of arms the tinctures by letters (e.g. a for argent and so on).

Index of Manuscripts

Additional

9016–19, 9021–2 (Anstis colls.), 22

19828–65 (Betham colls.), 22

22292–305 (armorial coffin-plates), 22

23683–7 (Betham colls.), 22

26677 (Powell's Roll), 25

28842–53 (Young colls.), 22

29502 ([Third] Calais Roll), 8, 25

31890 (Weston pedigree), 27

33244 (Furness Coucher Book II), 24

35213 (Chaloner catalogue), 13

37340 (Writhe's Garter Book [Hatton-Dugdale facs.]), 25, Pl. 11

37687 (grants of arms), 27

38537 (Dering (A) Roll), 9, 25

39249 (grant of arms to Sir Nicholas Bacon), 27, Pl. 14

39758 (Peterborough Roll), 8, 23, 24, Pl. 2

40078 (1515 Parliament Roll), 25

40742 (Fenn's Book of Badges), 24

40851 (Thomas Jenyns' Book [Qu. Margaret's Version]), 9, 17. Pl. 5

44026 (Hesketh of Rufford pedigree), 27

45130 (Luttrell Psalter), 26–27

45131 (Wriothesley's Funeral Colls.), 25, Pl. 12

45132 (Wriothesley's Standards, Fenwick A), 22, 25, Pl. IV

45133 (Salisbury Roll, etc.; Sir Thomas Holme's Book II), 10, 22, 25, Pl. 13

46354 (Writhe's Book of Knights), 22, 25

46920–47213 (Egmont Papers), 23

47979–83, 47990–3 (Martin Leake Papers), 23

48343 (Lyte Pedigree), 27

48976 (Rous Roll), 10, 25–26, Pl. III

Arundel

59 (arms of Thomas Wall), 20

71 (arms of Margaret of York, Duchess of Burgundy), 20

74 (Henry le Despenser's arms), 20

119 (William de la Pole's arms), 20

130 (Henry Percy's arms), 20

366, 435, 454, 461 (Card. Morton's arms), 20

Cotton

Caligula A.xviii (Caerlaverock Poem), 8, 13, Pl. 1

Caligula B.ii, iii (Benolt letters), 14

Claudius D.ii, 20

Claudius D.vi (Matthew Paris), 7, 13

Claudius E.viii, 13, 20

Cleoparta C.iii (Atkinson's Roll [Thynne's copy]), 13

Cleopatra C.iv (Benolt letters), 14

Cleopatra E.viii (Cottonian Roll), 13

Faustina E.i, 12, 14

Julius C.iii, 13

Julius C.vii, 12

Julius E.iv, 13

Nero A.ii, 20

Nero C.iii (Upton's 'De Officio Militari'), 14, Pl. 8

Nero D.i (Matthew Paris), 8, 13

Roll XV.8 (Camden Roll), 8, 12

Egerton

2581 B (grant of arms to John Parker), 27

2850 (Boroughbridge Roll), 24

3310 A (Philipot's Kentish church notes), 27, Pl. 16

3510 (Burton's Leicestershire church notes), 27

3713 (Willement's Roll), 9, 24, Pl. II

Harley
  337 (Harleian Roll), 8, 11, Pl. 3
  521 (Portcullis' Book), 11, Pl. 6
  1141, 10
  1163, 10
  1165, 10
  1197 (Card. Wolsey's arms), 20
  1408 (Aktinson's Roll [Penson's copy]), 13
  1499 (Tonge's Northern Visitation), 11
  1864, 21
  1979, 13, 14
  2169 (Randle Holme's Book), 10
  2259 (Strangways' Book), 12, Pl. 7
  2639 (John Tiptoft's arms), 20
  2900 (Oldhall Hours), 20, Pl. 9
  3862 (de Vere arms), 21
  4205 (Sir Thomas Hoeme's Book I), 9, 10, 11, *front cover*, Pl. I.
  4632 (Barker's Grants), 11
  4900, 11
  5829 (Philipot armorial bookstamp), 21
  6163 (Peter Le Neve's Book), 11
  6589 (Falkirk Roll), 8
  7025 (grants of arms), 11

Lansdowne
  285, 21
  689, 23
  857 (Dugdale's Staffs. Visitations), 19
  860 A, B (Henry Ferrers' colls.), 19
  861, 19

872 (Segar's Funerals), 19
880 (Leigh's Oxfordshire Visitation), 19
886–99, 908–18, 923 (Warburton's Yorkshire colls.), 19

Royal
  14 C.vii (Matthew Paris), 7, 15
  16 F.ii (royal arms of Henry VII), 21
  17 D.xx (Sir William Le Neve's arms), 21, Pl. 15
  18 A.xii (Anne Neville's arms), 21
  20 A.iv (royal arms of Henry VIII), 21

Sloane
  1301 (Second Dunstable Roll), 14

Stowe
  440 (Sir Edward Walker's colls.), 17
  580 (Sir Edward Walker's colls.), 17
  594 (Bruges' Garter Book), 9, 16–17, Pl. 10
  601 (Henry Chitting's colls.), 18
  633 (Anstis's autobiography), 18
  665, 666 (Anstis's 'Aspilogia'), 18
  668 (Glover's heraldic colls.), 18
  692 (alphabet of arms), 17
  696 (Thomas Jenyns' Book [Glover-Flower copy]), 9, 17
  749 (letters to Anstis), 18
  1045 (Francis Tate's colls.), 18
  1047 (Francis Thynne's commonplace-book), 18

32

Oncore i fui ie conoiffans · Johan de Bar li vurec
J or fa banicre barrec · De argent e de afur entaillic
O bende rouge engreellie · E guillemes de Cantelo
Ree ie par cefte raifon lo · Ree en honnour a touz ceuf veſti
feſſe baur or el rouge eſai · De trois flours de lis de or eſpars
flauſſins de teſtes de lupars · E puis huc de aportemer ·
Ei bien fe fanoir fere amer · O deuf feſſes de fair lenoir
La baniere Ree rouge anoir · eyes a Symon de mont agu
Ei anoir baniere e eſai · De ſnde au griffoun rampanr de or fin ·

Al quarte eſchiele o fon conroi · Couduit Edelbars li fielz le roy
Jouenceaus de diſ e ſet aus · e de nouuel armes portans ·
De cors fu beaus z aliſniez · De cuer courtois z enſeigniez
E deſirans de ben trouuer · On penſt fa force eſprouuer ·
Si cheuauchoir merueilles bel · E portoir o vn bleu label ·
Les armes le bon roi fon pere · Or li doinſ dieus grace Ree il pere ·
Auſi vaillans z non paſ meins · Lors portoir chaur eu fes meins ·
Tel Ree uel becnr ſaue oeu · Li preus Johans de fauir Johan
fu par conr o lui aſſemblans · Ku ſur tour fes guarnemens blans
El chief rouge or de or deus molectez · Blanche core z blanche alecz
Efcu blanc z baniere blanche · portoir o la vermeille manche
Rolers de bouz · Ru bien figue · Ree il eſt du cheualer au cigue
Baniere or Henris li tyois · plus blanche de vn poli lyois ·
O vn cheuron vermeil ennu · prouefce Ree anoir fait ſtu
De Guilleme le latimier · Ru la crois patee de or mier
portoir en rouge bien pourtraire · Sa baniere or cele part traire
Guillemes de leybourne · auſi vaillans homs · ſanz · meſ z ſmz · ſi
Baniere i or o largef paus · De ſnde o fis blans lyouns rampans
E puis rogiers de mortemer · Ru bela mer z dela mer
Al porte quel part Ree aur ale · Lefou barre au chief pale ·
E les corneres gyronnees · De or z de afur enluminees
O le efcuchon vndie de ermine · O noce les autres fe achemine
Car il z li denaur nomez · Alu filz le roy fureur remez ·
De ſon fren · Eujour · z Guardein · eyes oment Ree ie lef ordein ·

1. Caerlaverock Poem (or Roll). *Circa* 1300

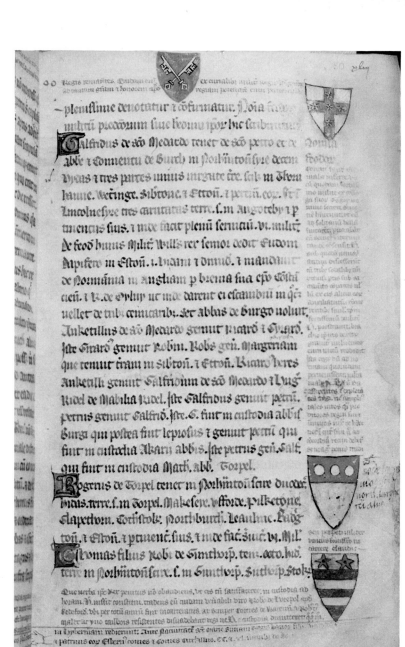

2. Peterborough Roll. *Circa* 1321–9

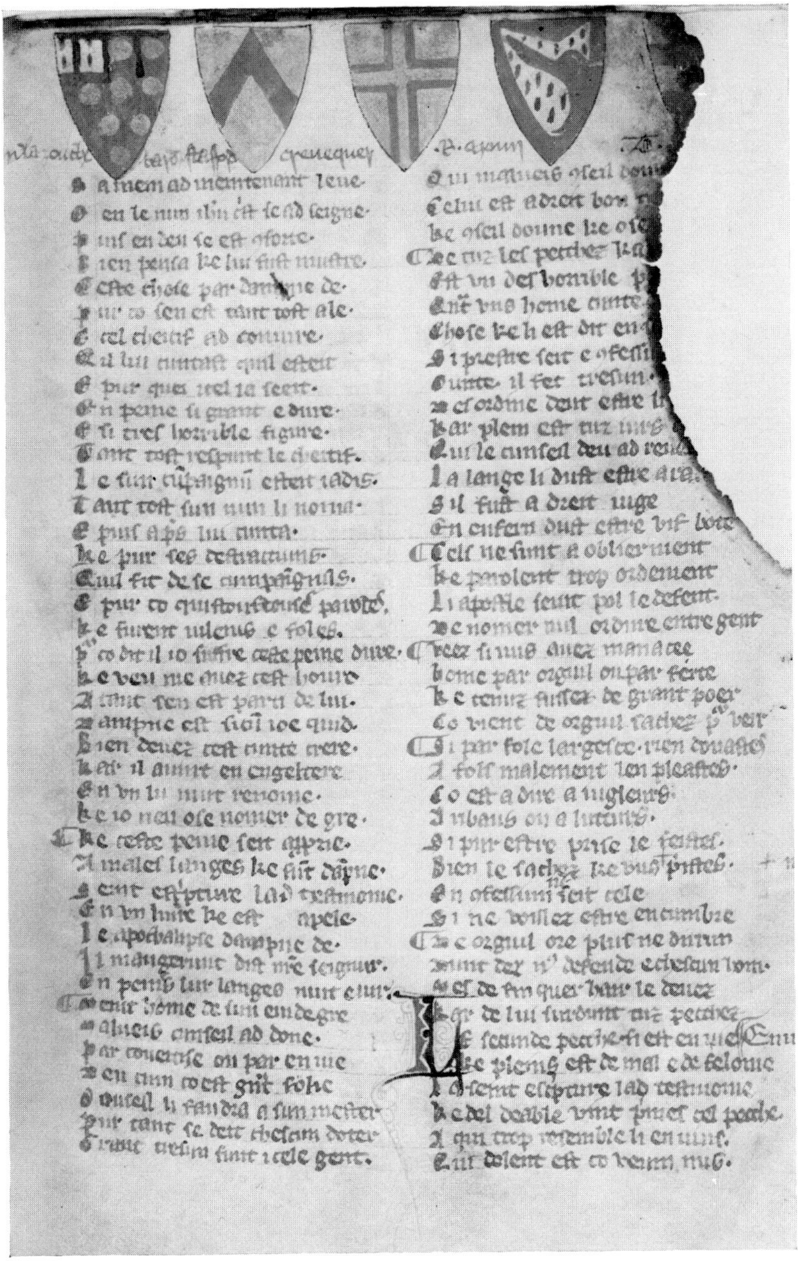

3. Harleian Roll. *Temp.* Edward II

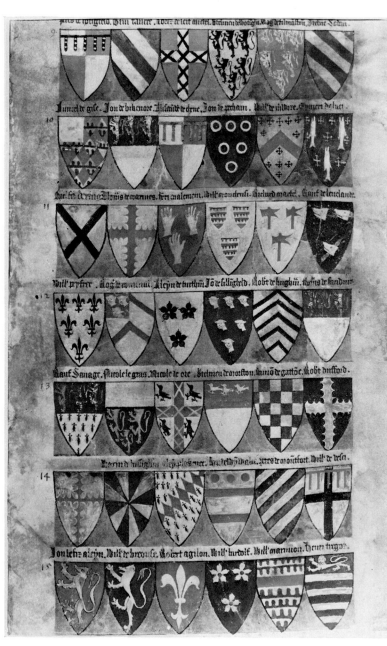

4. Dering (A) Roll, compiled *circa* 1275. Fifteenth-century *copy*

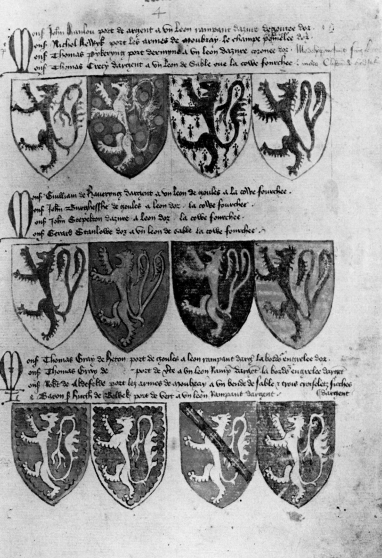

5. Thomas Jenyns' Book: Queen Margaret's Version. *Circa* 1440

6. Portcullis' Book. *Circa* 1440

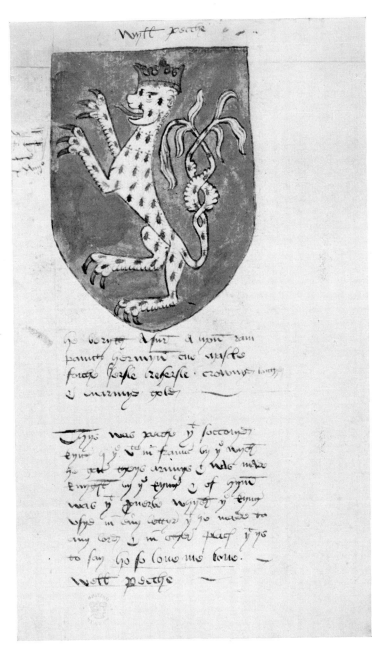

7. Richard Strangways' Book. Shield of arms of Sir William Pecche. Before 1488

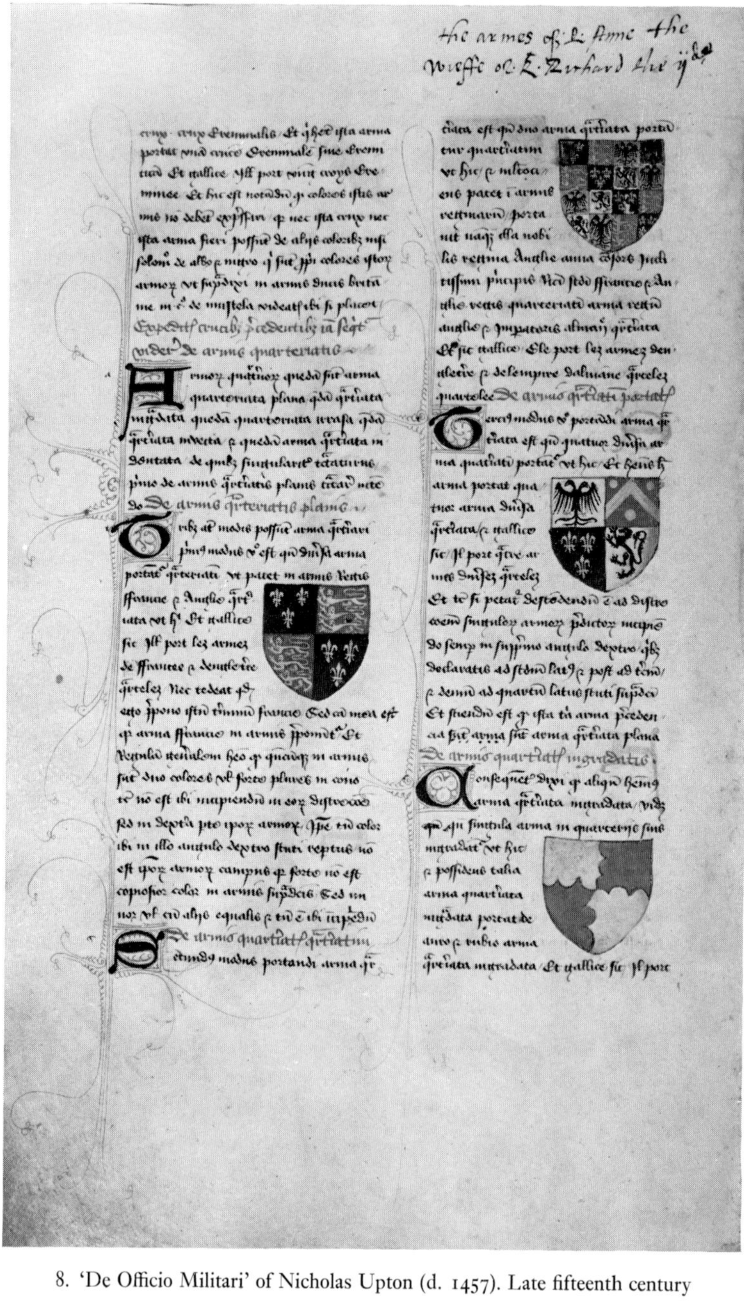

8. 'De Officio Militari' of Nicholas Upton (d. 1457). Late fifteenth century

Foigi martir
an dire. te deret
laus et gloria
predotatum

9. Book of Hours executed for Sir William Oldhall (d. ? 1466) and his wife, Margaret.
Mid-fifteenth century

10. Bruges' Garter Book. *Circa* 1430

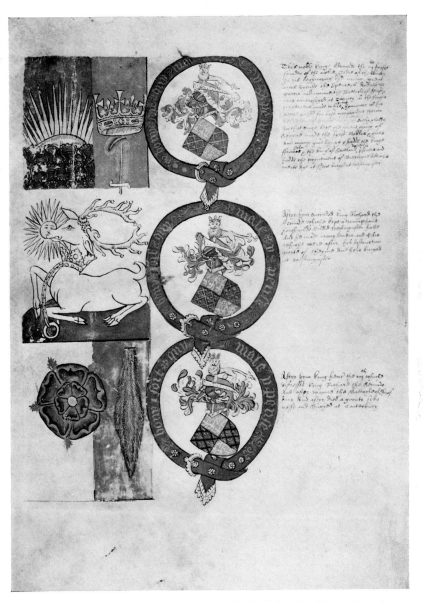

11. Writhe's Garter Book. *Facsimile copy* made for Sir Christopher Hatton, *circa* 1640

On the 19 day of [...] the 19 yere of our soveraign lord kyng
[...] the eight [...] at [...] the lord Willm conteny
Erll of Devonshire [...] had the kyngs [...] patents of erll
[...] [...] before he died, yet was he not creat
that notwithstanding the kyng for [...] favors as he [...] by
to hym [...] hym to bee buryed as an erll and commanded
by [...] of his [...] that he should bee named erll
for whom it was [...] in maner folowyng.

The body was [...] and remayned still in his [...] which
was [...] in the court on to the thursday [...] day of the [...]
month which at [...] none well accompanyed was to a
barge therfor [...] hanyng [...] bargemen for their [...]
and [...] and so by water was conveyed to [...] wharff.

12. Funeral collections of Sir Thomas Wriothesley, Garter King of Arms 1505–34

13. Salisbury Roll, compiled *circa* 1460. *Copy temp.* Richard III

14. Grant of arms to Sir Nicholas Bacon (d. 1579), Lord Keeper; 27 February 1568/9

15. Signatures and shield of arms of Sir William Le Neve as York Herald, 1625–33, in a manuscript formerly in his possession

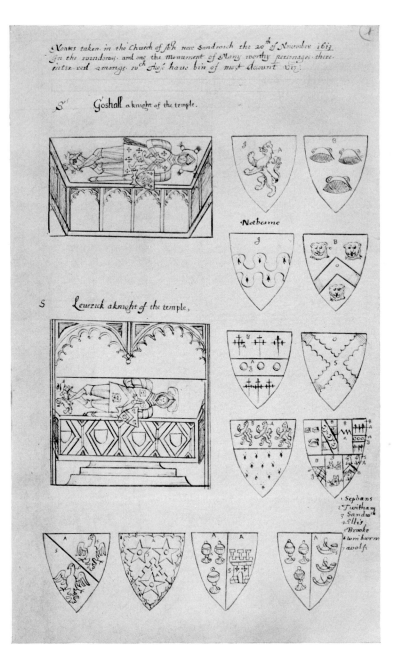

16. Notes and drawings of monuments and shields of arms in St. Nicholas's church at Ash-next-Sandwich, Kent, by John Philipot, 1613